RELIGIONS OF HUMANITY
PLAZA

Chelsea House Publishers
1974 Sproul Road, Suite 400
Broomall, PA 19008

The Chelsea House world wide web
address is www.chelseahouse.com

English-language edition
© 2002 by Chelsea House Publishers,
a subsidiary of Haights Cross
Communications

First Printing

1 3 5 7 9 6 4 2

Right: The Tree of Jesse is the genealogical chart which traces the Holy Family and Christ's lineage to the origins of Israel. It represents the process leading to the Incarnation of the Son of God. This sculptural representation of the Tree comes from a 16th-century retable from the chapel of Ormeau in southern France.

Opposite: Pilgrims arriving at the cathedral of Santiago in Spain. Since the middle ages, together with Rome and Jerusalem, this cult center on the Atlantic coast, which preserves the remains of St James (hence the name Santiago), has been one of the three major Christian centers of pilgrimage. Europe is criss-crossed with pilgrim routes and dotted with cult centers in honor of St James. The last decades of the second millennium have seen a resurgence in pilgrimages to Santiago by Catholics from all over Europe.

Library of Congress Cataloging-in-Publication Data Applied For:
ISBN: 0-7910-6624-X

© 2000 by
Editoriale Jaca Book spa, Milan
Originally published by
Editoriale Jaca Book, Milan, Italy

Design
Jaca Book

Original French text by
Julien Ries

JULIEN RIES

THE SCOPE OF
CATHOLICISM

CHELSEA HOUSE PUBLISHERS
PHILADELPHIA

CONTENTS

Easter Island, or Rapa Nui for the local inhabitants, lies in the middle of the South Pacific off the Chilean coast. The culture of Rapa Nui forms part of Pacific civilizations. Its encounter with Christianity took place in the seventeenth century, marking the first contact of the population with any other people for over a millennium. Christianity was accepted because it assimilated many of the local customs. The art of Rapa Nui maintains a peculiar and long-established style, as is shown by this effigy of the Virgin and Child from the church of the sole village on the island.

INTRODUCTION

In 410, following the sack of Rome by Alaric's Barbarian hordes and the subsequent Vandal invasions, Christianity looked on in dismay at the collapse of the empire and the dissolution of the Greco-Roman world. A melting pot of cultures, the Church resumed its evangelical mission. The baptism of Clovis by St. Remigius in Reims, and that of Ethelbert by St. Augustine in Canterbury, assured the conversion of Gaul and England to Christianity. The acceptance of the Gospel by the Barbarians gradually led these peoples toward the emergence of the Carolingian empire, rightly termed *regnum Christianitatis* (Christian kingdom), although feudal lordship came to exert undue power over local hierarchies. The foundation of the abbeys of Cluny (910) and Cîteaux (1098), which ushered in the Cistercian reform, projected the Rule of St. Benedict, signaling a new vitality. This period of renewed growth expressed itself in an unprecedented increase in the number of monasteries throughout Europe, a reform movement lead by Pope Gregory VII, the construction of Romanesque churches, and a surge of pilgrimages throughout the eleventh and the twelfth centuries. Indeed, the thirteenth century, with its Gothic cathedrals, its universities, its scholarship, and the rise of chivalry, which sublimated the warring spirit of the nobility, could well be described as the zenith of medieval Catholicism.

After an ebb in this dynamic impetus, sixteenth-century Europe enjoyed an extraordinary awakening during the Renaissance, a movement which began in Italy. This revival was characterized by a re-appraisal of the humanities, a return to classical influences, sweeping geographic exploration, the invention of printing, and advances in the arts, literature, and the sciences. This renewal was vigorously sustained by a humanistic papacy, but was offset by the resultant pagan tendencies that swept over Rome. Although these movements were counterbalanced by the appearance of a host of Christian humanists, the Church was eventually challenged by the ideas of Luther, Calvin, and Henry VIII. Protestantism unleashed a veritable earthquake that produced a catastrophic breach within Christianity. Catholicism responded with the Council of Trent, which issued momentous changes, and effectively implemented a range of needed reforms. Still other challenges loomed large over the horizon in the form of absolutism, the Enlightenment, and political revolutions. Although a sense of alarm characterized the period between the seventeenth and the nineteenth centuries, Catholicism thrived through an aggressive missionary program that continued throughout the nineteenth century in Asia, Africa, and America. During this period, the Church also drew strength from the foundation of new religious congregations, a flourishing of charitable enterprises, and the consolidation of social Catholicism. Two world wars in the twentieth century left in their wake a devastated world that cried for reconstruction. The Church again rose to the occasion. The Second Vatican Council, convened in 1962 by John XXIII and closed in 1965 by Paul VI, instilled a great sense of hope in the Church and in believers throughout the world: hope in a unity between churches, and harmony among nations — a true *Gaudium et Spes*. Not since 1439, when the Church tried in vain to reunite its Catholic and Orthodox branches and heal the schism that had kept them apart since 1054, had such a dramatic move toward unification been made.

An open-air gathering in Manila, Philippines, in 1986 on the occasion of democratic elections, following the fall of the oppressive post-war dictatorial regime. Note the sisters and religious in the front row, united with the rest of the population in a commitment toward the realization of a more equitable social fabric.

CATHOLICISM TODAY

The term Catholic (universal) denotes a fundamental characteristic of the Christian faith. Historically it defines the Christian Church, which recognizes the primacy of the pope (the bishop of Rome), as distinct from the other Christian denominations — Orthodox, Anglican, or Protestant. These denominations developed from the as yet unresolved tensions that erupted first between the East and the West toward the close of the first millennium, and later within the West itself throughout the second millennium. Fortunately the dawn of the twentieth century saw the emergence of an ecumenical dialogue that, on the basis of a common heritage, tried to re-establish the Church's original unity. Introduced by Pope John XXIII (1958-1963), and implemented by Popes Paul VI (1963-1978) and John Paul II, Vatican Council II (1962-1965) projected to the world an image of a Church that is sensitive to the needs of mankind, respectful of human liberty, in tune with man's initiatives, supportive of his anguish, and of service to his aspirations. The frequent inter-continental travels of Pope John Paul II have exercised a great attraction among many peoples and have contributed greatly toward the maintenance of harmony and stability among nations.

During the second half of the twentieth century the Catholic Church was hit by the repercussions of a global crisis resulting from several factors: the grievous consequences of two tragic wars, the deportations and movement of entire populations, the demographic explosion of newly independent nations, the technological race of the industrialized countries, and the attempt by once underdeveloped states to attain the highest cultural achievements. An increasing secularization — as well as the influence of new ideologies and the debate over priority between development, humanization, and evangelization — led to a dearth of vocations and to a weakening of religious practice in the West.

In response, the Catholic Church has intensified its ecumenical, inter-religious, and inter-cultural dialogues. Great attempts have been made for the inculturization of the Gospel within Western society and within the varied and ethnic cultures of Latin America, Africa, and Asia, where the young Churches are very active. The emergence and rapid expansion of new religious movements and communities has been quite remarkable. Invited to Rome on Pentecost eve, on May 30, 1998, 350,000 adherents of these movements heeded Pope John Paul II's exhortation to a coordinated worldwide commitment of the Church in the service of humanity.

At the dawn of the third millennium, the Catholic Church offers to many the greatest of hopes – through its hierarchy and its social teaching, through its solicitude toward the individual, and through the impact of its Christian anthropology, which remains grounded in the mystery of the Incarnation and in the Gospel message.

4. Ecumenical meeting at Assisi in October 1986. Pope John Paul II poses for photographers with representatives of Christian denominations and of different religions. Towards the end of the second millennium, Catholicism continued to explore ways for cultural exchanges among religions, with the intention of reciprocal enrichment. As the savior of the whole world, Christ is present within the different cultures and these could draw mutual support and nourishment from each other.

1. 2. Preparations for the festivity of the Assumption, August 15, 1998, at the church of Tonantzintla on the Mexican highlands. Fruits and flowers, sign of God's benevolence on mankind, echo the traditional culture of the Indios who formerly implored their gods for rain and rich harvests. On the eve of the festivity, the effigy of the Virgin is placed at the foot of the altar, at the end of a long carpet of flowers. The effigy is displayed lying down in the tradition of the Dormition of the Virgin, and is then exhibited in a standing position on the day of the Assumption.

3. *The façade of the church of Tonantzintla. Its architecture, rich in color and ornament, is the product of popular art, the expression of a Christianity which appreciates local traditions.*

THE SPREAD OF CATHOLICISM

Prevalence of Catholics

Prevalence of Christians

Catholics within
predominantly Christian areas

Significant Christian presence

Significant Catholic and
Christian presence

Significant presence of Catholics

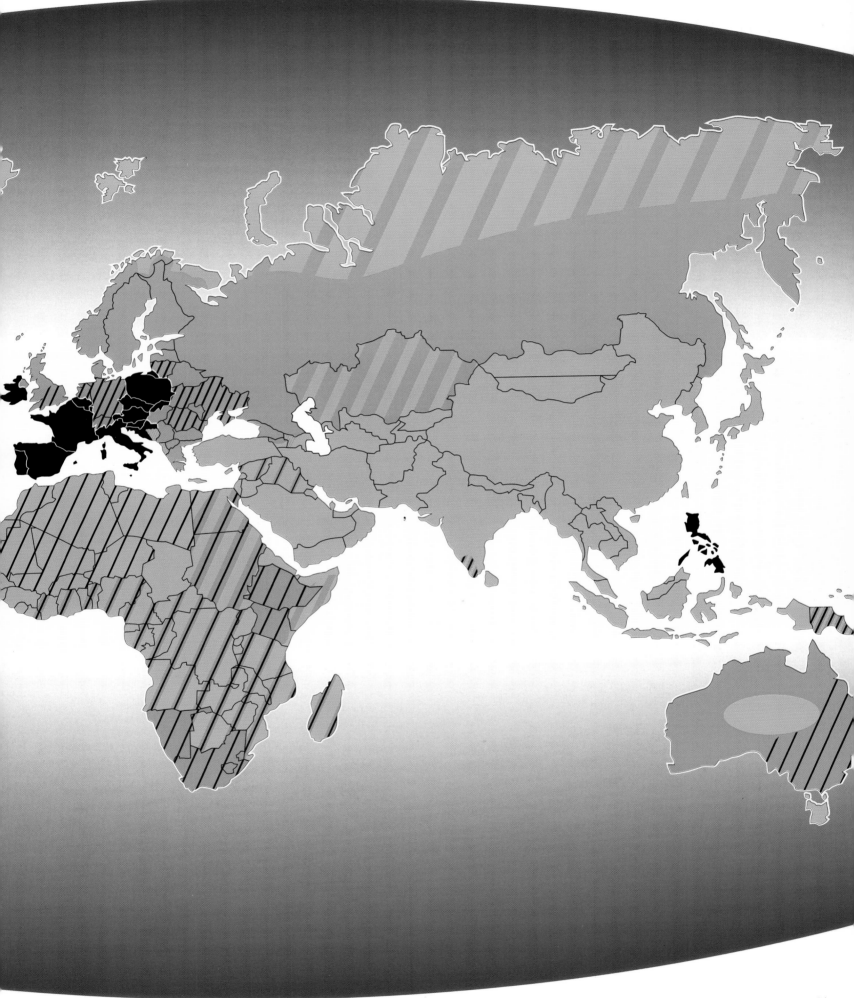

3
THE MAKING OF A POPULAR RELIGION
The Conversion of Western Europe

1. *St. Benedict in a miniature preserved at Monte Cassino, Italy. Benedictine monasteries not only acted as religious centers, but as stimuli for the renewal of the cultural life and the economy of the Middle Ages.*

On August 24, 410, Alaric, king of the Visigoths, occupied Rome, a city recently devastated by his hordes. Now under Barbarian rule, the empire was gripped by alarm. Yet, being a melting pot of cultures, the Church continued with its work — restoring cathedrals and sanctuaries and pursuing its evangelical mission. After being crowned king of the Franks in 481, Clovis and three thousand soldiers converted to Christianity, establishing themselves in Paris and transforming Gaul into 'the eldest daughter of the Church.' In collaboration with monks from Lerins, Spain, and Africa, itinerant bishops went on to evangelize town and countryside. Theodoric the Great (d. 526), founder of the Ostrogoth kingdom in Italy, adopted the old administrative machinery of Rome, bringing together Catholics and Arians in a synthesis that remains amply reflected in such monuments as those at Ravenna. Toward the year 540 St. Benedict of Nursia compiled his Rule, which became the centerpiece of monasticism in Gaul.

It was, however, under that adept promoter of Christian thought, Pope Gregory the Great (592-604), that the fusion between Roman tradition and Barbarian vitality was completed. He injected new vigor into the evangelization of the countryside — attending to the ordination of priests, and the establishment of episcopal or presbyteral teaching centers. He supported the work of monastic schools and distinguished himself among the founders of popular medieval religious life. Enhancement of civilization was a goal so strongly grounded within the Church that the papacy became 'a veritable rallying point for the Barbarian West' (Guy Bédouelle). In an age of a simple yet formidable faith, Barbarian society produced innumerable saints. Pope Gregory had instructed the monks whom he had sent to England to '…destroy the idols but to preserve the temples.' His was indeed an authentic desire for an inculturation of the Gospel that would have profound repercussions on pagan peoples.

In Italy the Longobard invasion put such pressure on the Church that numerous monks and priests emigrated northward into Europe. Meanwhile, in sixth-century Ireland, the Church flourished by projecting itself from monasteries as centers of faith. From Ireland St. Columbanus traveled into Scotland and from there, with twelve companions, arrived in Gaul, where he founded Luxeuil and undertook the evangelization of northern Europe. As a result, national Churches sprang up, giving rise to a popular Christianity that nourished itself from Benedictine centers, which radiated peace, stability, and the valorization of work. This was indeed the birth of Christian Europe, which owed its origins to Benedictine monks from Italy and to the monks of St. Columbanus from Ireland.

2. *An artist's impression of an 8th-century European village. The parish churches with their monasteries were the focal point of the communities; the parish school provided the best education for the people.*
3. *Map of Europe, showing the route followed by the 6th-century Irish missionary monks in their Christianization of the continent. Though they were the last of the western Europeans to embrace Christianity, the Irish went back to a Europe in crisis following the fall of the Roman empire. The map shows the famous route covered by St. Columbanus between the end of the 6th and the beginning of the 7th century. Along this route he established an impressive number of monasteries. The most famous were those of Luxeuil in France and Bobbio in Italy.*
4. *The ruins of the ancient monastery of Skellig Michael in southern Ireland.*

The uncial superimposed over Ireland is taken from the 'Cathach,' a 7th-century illuminated codex belonging to St. Columba, the mentor of St. Columbanus.

ITALY

SWITZERLAND
Bobbio

Zürich
Luxeuil

FRANCE

Canterbury

ENGLAND

IRELAND

Bangor

Iona

SCOTLAND

THE CHURCH AND THE CHALLENGES OF HISTORY
Christianity between Feudalism and Empire

Under the Carolingians, the Church experienced momentous changes. In 732 Charles Martel stopped the Muslims at Poitiers, eventually forcing them back across the Pyrenees. Later, Martel's grandson, Charlemagne, restored order within society and in 800 was crowned emperor by Pope Leo III in Rome. His collaborator, Alcuin, introduced Anglo-Saxon scholarship into Frankish schools and served as one of the great contributors toward a new awakening in literature, the arts, and theology. The Church contributed greatly to this era of peace and the accompanying cultural revival has been aptly termed the 'Carolingian Renaissance.' The emperor considered himself responsible for Christianity and its cohesion as guaranteed by dogma and the Roman liturgy. He saw to the nomination of bishops and regarded himself as both the custodian of doctrine and the defender of faith.

Toward the end of the ninth century, with the dissolution of the empire and the arrival of the Germanic emperors (Otto I was crowned Holy Roman Emperor in 962), the Church found itself at the mercy of feudal lords, who claimed for themselves exclusive rights to nominate bishops and administer ecclesiastical property. Throughout the tenth century, these feudal lords opposed the power of the papacy. Dioceses and parishes came to be offered to the highest bidder, and decay swept over the ranks of both the clergy and laypersons. It was from the model monastery at Cluny,

founded in 910, that the so-called Gregorian reform was implemented. Its name derives from the Cluniac monk who was elected pope as Gregory VII in 1073. This pope re-affirmed papal primacy, dispatched legates to enforce clerical celibacy, and prohibited the emperor from further nominations of bishops. When Emperor Henry IV deposed the archbishop of Milan, Gregory VII excommunicated him until he presented himself in penitential garb at Canossa. The conflict was only settled in 1182 by the Concordat of Worms between Pope Callixtus II and Emperor Henry V, which emphasized the distinction between Church and state and affirmed the primacy of the spiritual power of the Church.

The twelfth century was a dynamic time for western Christianity. It was an era that witnessed special contacts with the East, a campaign of Crusades, and a revival of holiness and learning in which the universal use of Latin guaranteed the unity of Europe. Thanks to the influence of Cluny, the Rule of St. Benedict was adopted by almost all monasteries. Romanesque churches were built — houses of God for community and pilgrims, and the meeting place for God and man. Renowned for its pilgrimages and the veneration of saints and relics, the twelfth century is best remembered for its Romanesque symbolism, which drew its inspiration from the Bible and the universe, and helped introduce man to the mysteries of religious faith.

1. 4. Two artistic impressions showing the transformations carried out by the great Benedictine monastic movement which radiated from the abbey of Cluny in France. **Left:** *a typical European rural area in a ruinous state, after the crisis of the Carolingian world in the 10th Century.* **Right:** *St. Miguel de Cuxa in Spain, where the monastic movement brought new life.*
2. Miniature from the codex of Mathilda of Canossa (1066-1115) depicting this great woman of the medieval world engaged in reconciling Emperor Henry the IV with Pope Gregory VII, obliging the former to beg pardon for his arrogance (Vatican Apostolic Library, Rome).

3. The belfry-tower of the great abbey at Cluny.

CHRIST RECAPITULATES THE CREATION
The Great Centuries of Medieval Christianity

'Blessed be life under the crozier!' This popular medieval dictum encapsulates the social and religious sentiments prevalent in the twelfth and thirteenth centuries. People started to migrate into the countryside from nearby castles and monasteries, which had offered them shelter in times of invasion. These migrations, combined with the heavy demographic expansion of these two centuries, gave birth to the great European cities. The Church sublimated the belligerent spirit of the chivalric orders, directing them toward mystical ideals as exemplified in the legendary quest for the Holy Grail. Thousands came forward to join in the Crusades with the intention of holding back the Muslim invaders and securing freedom for Christians in the Holy Land. This movement was animated by St. Bernard of Clairvaux (1091-1153), whose reform of Cîteaux propagated a spirit of evangelical poverty, the principal exponents of which were St. Dominic and St. Francis of Assisi and their followers.

The image of Christ enthroned in glory came to dominate the portals and the stained-glass windows of Gothic cathedrals, where the high and sprightly vaults seem to reach into the skies in reflection of cosmic harmony. These cathedrals – particularly those at Chartres, Bourges, and Reims – created spaces of light, blending a complexity of features into a harmonious unity and leading man toward his Creator. Throughout the thirteenth century, universities of learning grew in number and served as symbols of scientific fervor reflecting the development of wisdom and progress. The Church was the prime mover behind these institutions, injecting new vitality into the study of theology and philosophy and into the education of priests and the faithful. *Summae*, or comprehensive treatises, made their appearance in the thirteenth century, and include the noted work by St. Thomas Aquinas (1235-1274), which was based on a coherent and comprehensive system of philosophy that embraced within it the teachings of Aristotle as rediscovered by the Arabs. The life of the Church was anchored within the theology of creation and the incarnation, and was further nourished by the cult of saints and the phenomenon of pilgrimages. In 1274 the Second Council of

1. Main portal of the cathedral at Chartres in France. The figure of Christ lies in the center, surrounded with the symbols of the evangelists. In Romanesque and Gothic portals the Son of God is very often surrounded by figures from the Old and the New Testaments. In Christ, history and the whole of creation acquire their meaning.
2. 3. Two low reliefs from the portal of the cathedral at Auxerre in France, depicting the creation of Adam and that of Eve from one of Adam's ribs.

Lyon made efforts to reconcile eastern and western Christianity.

Further divisions and ruptures shook western Christianity in the fourteenth and fifteenth centuries. The dualistic heresies of the Bogomils, the Albigenses, and the Cathars drove the Church to establish the Inquisition, a tribunal created to supervise matters of faith and to lead people back to the Church. Challenges to papal power forced Pope Clement V to seek refuge in Avignon (1309), marking the prelude to the Great Western Schism. From 1337 to 1453 an interminable war between England and France helped spread plague and terror. The threat of laicism, which aimed to subject the Church to temporal power, ushered in an era of secularization. The people of God rallied against this challenge with expressions of faith that included the cult of Christ Incarnate, called *Devotio Moderna*, as exemplified in the feast of *Corpus Christi* and *The Imitation of Christ*; the recitation of the Holy Rosary; the doctrine of the Assumption of the Virgin; numerous confraternities; the cult of saints and national heroes like Joan of Arc in France and Nicholas of Flue in Switzerland; and the veneration of charismatic figures like Raymond Lull (d. 1315) and Nicholas of Cusa (d. 1464) — all of whom were imbued with a great sense of Catholicism.

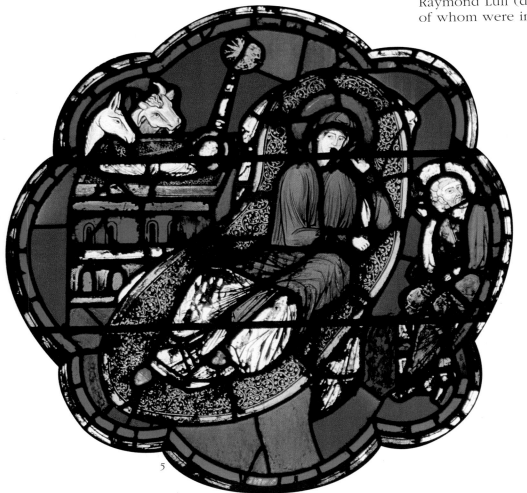

4. In the 13th century, the Order of the Dominican friar preachers dedicated itself to the teaching of the Christian faith in the expanding cities. City life was considered a distraction and every effort was made to make man more conscious of his destiny.

5. A Gothic stained-glass window from the cathedral of Lyon depicting the nativity of Christ. The ass and the ox which kept him warm in the manger represent all the people of the world who turn to Christ.

THE DAWN OF CHRISTIAN HUMANISM
The Church and the Challenge of Renaissance

1

Decimated by decades of war and plague and exhausted by emerging national rivalries, man yearned for a change. The achievements of Giotto (1266-1337), Boccaccio (1313-1375), and Petrarch (1304-1375) brought a surge of renewal over Italy. The decisive event was the Council of Florence, convened in 1439 to bring together the east and the west. The Byzantine faction, led by Cardinal Bessarione, obtained unexpected success and generated genuine enthusiasm among the westerners. Latins and Greeks drew closer together following the fall of Constantinople to the Turks in 1453, just before the Platonic Academy was established at the court of the Medicis in Florence. This institution ushered in the Italian Renaissance, which soon spread throughout Europe, fueled by wealth, patronage, and the invention of printing.

During this period, new horizons unfolded before western Christianity. In 1492 the Spanish *Reconquista* against Islam was completed with the victory at Granada, while on October 12 Christopher Columbus set foot on the Bahamas in the Caribbean, at the same time that Portugal explored the coast of Africa. The papacy was elated. Julius II and Paul III commissioned Bramante and Michelangelo to rebuild the basilica of St. Peter. A series of humanistic popes patronized the arts and transformed Rome into a new city, influenced by the mythology and deities of pagan antiquity. This new Roman paganism and corruption led Fra Girolamo Savonarola to denounce Pope Alexander VI.

In 1485 Pico della Mirandola published his famous theses, which were preceded by an introductory text, *Oration on the Dignity of Man*. His was a veritable manifesto of Christian humanism, which looked upon Christ as the paragon of wisdom. Great humanists like Marsilio Ficino (1433-1499), Thomas More (1478-1535), and Erasmus (1466-1536) insisted on a return to the word of God, the Holy Bible, and Christ. Conscious of the pitfalls of paganism latent in the Renaissance, these scholars created a humanism based on the Gospel, and laid the foundations for the joining of Church and culture.

The discovery of new lands heralded an era of missionary activity, launched by a papal bull of Alexander VI in 1493. In America and Africa, the spread of Christianity did not encounter the organized structures found in the great religions of Asia. The collapse of local cults allowed the rapid conversion to Christianity of the peoples of Africa and the new Spanish-American world. In 1453 Nicholas of Cusa published his *The Peace of Faith*, a pioneering and thought-provoking work, which was the first to discuss the dialogue between Christianity and the various local cultures as conducted in Asia by St. Francis Xavier (1506-1552) and Matteo Ricci (d. 1620), and in America by Bartolomé de las Casas (d. 1556).

1. Though plagued with frequent wars, 15th-century Europe became increasingly wealthy.
2. Man discovered his ability for great undertakings and risked deluding himself that he no longer required God's constant support. Erasmus of Rotterdam, a man of great culture – shown here in a portrait by Dürer – saw human ingenuity as an incentive towards a constant relationship with God who is the origin of all wisdom.

2

3. Art saw the emergence of great architects. Brunelleschi is here shown directing works on the Cathedral of Santa Maria del Fiore at Florence, then perhaps the foremost center of European humanism.

4. In the 15th century the Europeans encountered with new worlds. The illustration depicts a Portuguese delegation paying homage to the king of Congo in Africa. The king's conversion to Christianity towards the end of the century led to the conversion of his sons and the rest of the great Congo Kingdom.

MISSIONS, CHARITY, AND MYSTICISM
The Church between Reform and Absolutism

In 1517 a German Augustinian friar named Martin Luther (1483-1546) began to teach about the need to purify the Church's beliefs. He refuted a number of dogmas and ignored the sacraments, except baptism and the Eucharist. His abandonment of tradition led to a great schism. Luther's teachings about this 'new faith' were adopted by the French layman John Calvin (1509-1564), who established a Protestant Church in Geneva. Except for pastors, this Church had no hierarchy and was based on a biblical Christology and a rigid morality. In England, Henry VIII established Anglicanism, a new religion that came between Catholicism and Protestantism.

With entire nations embracing Protestantism, the Catholic Church responded with a reform program that drew its inspiration from the three sessions of the Council of Trent (1545-1563). The conciliar decrees clearly re-affirmed the Catholic creed of scripture, tradition, justification, original sin, the holy sacrifice of the Mass, and the sacraments. The Council set in motion an ambitious program of reform insisting, among others, on the duty of residence for bishops and curates, priestly celibacy, the establishment of seminaries, the compilation of a catechism, missal, and breviary, as well as a renewal of preaching. Capuchins and Jesuits were enlisted to help the diocesan clergy in its pastoral work, especially in the German lands. The effect of these efforts began to be felt by the middle of the sixteenth century.

In 1555 the Treaty of Augsburg divided Europe into Catholic and Lutheran areas; while the Treaty of Westphalia, which concluded the Thirty Years War (1618-1648), added a 'Calvinist' faction to it. Jews were expelled from all countries, finding refuge only in the Papal States. Seventeenth-century Europe came to be dominated by state absolutism based on the principle of one king, one religion, and one law, and replacing the long-forgotten Christian unity of medieval times.

1. The Crucifixion by Velázquez (17th century) follows a different artistic trend. The triumphant Romanesque Christ is here substituted by a suffering one, to whom mystics turn in imitation of his sorrowful experience.

The Church was thus confronted with an establishment that tolerated no rivalry. In France Gallicanism vindicated the autonomy of the local Church in its differences with Rome, especially under Louis XIV. Fully conscious of their absolutism, the various states unreservedly reaffirmed the necessary unity of religion and nation.

The Church, however, made extensive progress both internally and externally. Religious life underwent a veritable and remarkable renewal under John of the Cross and Teresa of Avila in Spain; Charles Borromeo and Philip Neri in Italy; and the great founders Francis de Sales, Peter Berulle, Jean-Jacques Olier, and John Eudes in France. In combating political absolutism, the Church proposed absolute charity, embodied in such figures as Vincent de Paul, a naval chaplain who founded the Sisters of Charity. On June 22, 1622, Pope Gregory XV established the Congregation for the Propagation of Faith (*De Propaganda Fide*), which provided a new missionary impetus. Its instructions of 1659 demanded the establishment of an indigenous clergy, healthy relations with political rulers, and respect toward local traditions, populations, and customs — thus furthering inculturization of the Gospel.

5

6

2. In the 1400s the dukes of Bourgogne in France built the Hotel de Dieu in Beaune as a hospice and a hospital for the poor. It was a sumptuous building meant to cater for but a few of the many paupers who, in reality, were considered a nuisance by the rich and middle classes.
3. 4 In 17th-century France St. Vincent de Paul founded an effective organization to alleviate poverty in town and country. This movement came to embrace sisters and laity, and exercised considerable influence in subsequent centuries among Catholics.
5. 6. Photo and reconstruction of a building in Paraguay, dating back to the great missionary activity of the Jesuits in Latin America. Conscious of the havoc inflicted by European settlers through their exploitation of the Indios, the Jesuits tried to establish Christian communities which preserved local traditions, offered protection against exploitation, and allowed the Indios to live fraternally.

ENLIGHTENMENT, SECULARIZATION, AND PERSECUTION

The Church Confronted by Unbelief and Revolution

1

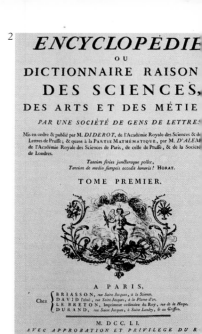

2

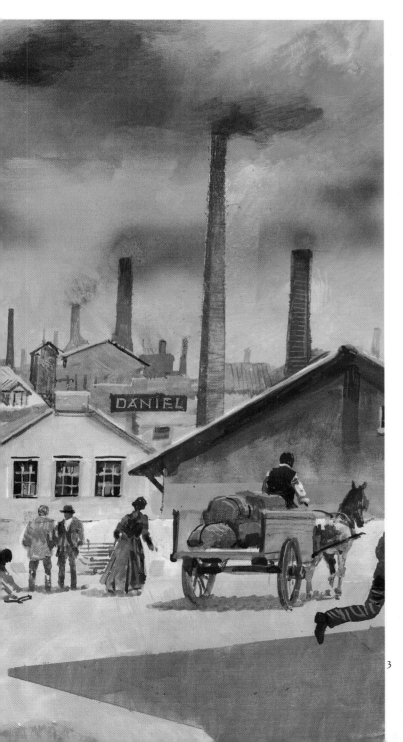

The eighteenth century distanced itself from the classicism of its predecessor and introduced European society to a new order of ideas and human relationships. The emergent middle classes brought with them a sharing of experiences, but their dominant egalitarianism led to a refutation of former traditions and privileges. In the absence of great Christian thinkers, public opinion came to be exclusively molded by the deistic philosophers such as Bayle and his *Dictionary*, Diderot and his *Encyclopedia*, Jean-Jacques Rousseau and his natural religion of purely sentimental content, Voltaire, and the French Masonic movement with its concept of God as the 'Great Architect of the Universe.' In the wake of the French Enlightenment, Lessing established himself as the head of the *Aufklärung*, the German version of the Enlightenment. Completely divested of the supernatural, religion was made to rely solely on reason, accepting Christ but excluding his divinity.

Catholicism was caught unaware by a similar intellectual revolution that infiltrated its ranks. Drawing from Fénelon's search into the perfect love of God, with its complete disregard of evil, the quietism of Madame Guyon developed into a false practice of Christian life. The formation of the clergy and the religious education of the masses left much to be desired. The Church was also shaken by the errors of Febronianism — a form of episcopalism that limited the primacy of the bishop of Rome to his particular diocese, transferred absolute primacy to a general council, and entrusted lay princes with the supervision over religious matters in their territories.

Influenced by the teachings of Voltaire, political Josephism secularized seminaries and religious orders, and even legislated liturgical matters. Mounting hostility toward the Jesuits increased to the extent that, for the sake of good order, Pope Clement XIV was compelled to suppress the Society of Jesus on July 21, 1773. Subsequently, founders of religious congregations appeared, including John Eudes, Grignion de Montfort, and Alphonse Maria de Liguori.

In 1789, the French Revolution erupted in a bloody whirlwind and produced a "religion" of ridiculous cults, such as that of the Goddess of Reason, its deistic tenets, and its cult of the Supreme Being. Christianity answered the challenge, retaliating with the Wars of the Vendée, the propagation of the cult of the Sacred Heart, and resistance to the Republic. The Church was, however, weakened by a veritable hemorrhage of anti-Catholic persecution, which included the massacre and deportation of clergy and the spoliation and pillaging of the Church's patrimony, which was destroyed and squandered. Church-State relations were only restored with a concordat between Napoleon and Pope Pius VII. Throughout the nineteenth century, following various national revolutions, a number of similar concordats were negotiated by the Church for the sake of its faithful. Following the upheaval of the Industrial Revolution, the Catholic Church preached a social Catholicism till then unknown, characterized by Frederick Ozanam, Don Giovanni Bosco, Wilhelm Ketteler, Cardinal Mermillod, and Leo XIII (*Rerum Novarum*). At the height of the colonial revolution the Church sought to preach Christ through a host of cathechists, teachers, medics, nurses, and instructors. One could indeed characterize the nineteenth century as the age of an authentic Catholic missionary epic.

THOUGHT, PRESENCE, AND ACTION
Catholicism and Modern Challenges

Throughout the nineteenth century the Church came face to face with the doctrine of Positivism, to which Pope Pius IX responded by summoning the First Vatican Council (1869-1870). The Council was brutally interrupted on September 20, 1870, by the invasion of Rome by the Italian army, in an attempt to annex the Papal States. The Church's declaration on papal infallibility on July 18, 1870, led to the *Kulturkampf*, the German empire struggle to control the Church, adopted later by Switzerland, France, and Italy. The victims of this anticlericalism, successor to the Enlightenment, were the religious congregations and religious instruction.

Despite such setbacks, the Church experienced a surge of vitality on many fronts, including its universities (Louvain, Dublin, Freiburg, and Paris); the Catholic press; an intellectual renewal lead by such authors as Newman and Mercier; and a return to patristic studies, biblical exegesis, analysis of Church history, and the study of non-Christian denominations (The Parliament of Religions at Chicago, 1893). Pope Leo XIII (1878-1903) opened new prospects with his insistence on the study of medieval sources of Christian thought, his promotion of social Catholicism (*Rerum Novarum*), and his renewed interest in the eastern churches. Many intellectuals from different

1. Print from the Civica Raccolta di Stampe *at Milan, showing the opening ceremony, on December 8, 1869, of Vatican Council I, convened on the initiative of Pius IX.*
2. Bismarck, the European statesman who promoted a policy of hostility towards Christian involvement in civil life.

3. 4. The young John Henry Newman and the Belgian Cardinal Mercier, great promoters of the relationship between faith and reason.
5. Pope Leo XIII.

quarters came to embrace Christianity, among them Bloy, Maritain, Psichari, Huysmans, Rouault, Péguy, and Claudel. Numerous religious and missionary congregations flourished, the latter addressing themselves specifically to spreading the faith in Asia and Africa. But the clash between Catholicism and the modern world led to the modernist crisis, with negative repercussions on the internal life of the Church.

After the First World War the Church increased in prestige among public opinion and world leaders. It was the era of concordats between Church and State. The Church also attained new freedom on the international platform with the creation of a Vatican City-State, which replaced the suppressed former Papal States. In the face of new ideologies, the Church re-affirmed the primacy of the spiritual; it increased its social and charitable enterprises and offered its support to literature and the arts. Pius XI (1922-1939) established Catholic Action, a movement that injected youth with a vitality that was to have significant effects on Church and society and that helped organize an elite Catholic corps. A brilliant and fearless pope, Pius XI vehemently condemned Nazism and Marxism as oppressors of the individual and society.

The global tragedy of 1940-1945 left millions of young victims on the battlefields. In its aftermath, in the context of two politically opposed politico-ideological blocs, Pope Pius XII (1939-1958) made extensive use of the media to address the world's faithful and to proclaim the great principles that regulate the individual, the family, society, and peace. The papacy thus established itself as an influential element of global opinion, at a time when a group of political leaders, bound together by a similar ideological program – De Gasperi, Adenauer, and Schuman – were applying themselves to the reconstruction of a devastated Europe. The great thinkers who laid the future of Catholicism include Congar, de Lubac, Journet, von Balthasar, Jungmann, and Teilhard de Chardin.

6. *Nazi poster proclaiming 'The Final Blow,' depicting the Nazi swastika crushing the Catholics and the red communists.*
7. *Soviet poster of the 1920s showing Lenin sweeping Russia clean of priests, crowned heads, and capitalists.*
8. *Pope Pius XI.*
9. *Pope Pius XII with the then Secretary of State Montini, the future Pope Paul VI, behind him.*

25

LIGHT FOR THE CHURCH, HOPE FOR THE WORLD
Vatican Council II

In 1959, with the western world enjoying an economic boom in the aftermath of post-war reconstruction, Pope John XXIII (d. 1963) announced 'a general council for the universal Church.' Launched on October 11, 1962, Vatican Council II worked through four sessions before its closure under Pope Paul VI (1963-1978) on December 8, 1965. Its sixteen decrees addressed the pressing problems of the Church and probed into its origins, constitution, organization, mission, and identity in the modern world. The Council, which was attended by 2,500 bishops from all the continents and by non-Catholic and lay observers, was a watershed for the Church and the world.

As a counterbalance to the ecclesiology of the First Vatican Council, the conciliar fathers defined episcopal collegiality, stressing the episcopate as a sacrament and the Church as a communion. The establishment of episcopal conferences became mandatory. Christian liturgy was highlighted as the expression of the salvific work carried on by the Church, and ensuring Christ's presence among God's people. The brief but rich text on religious liberty evaluated the dignity of man endowed with reason, will, and responsibility, and committed to the search of truth. The Council set in motion a dialogue between Catholics and other Christian and non-Christian denominations as well as with non-believers and the world at large. The documents that regulated these relationships were a novelty whose impact is still felt today. Their implementation was entrusted to pontifical secretariats specifically created by Pope Paul VI, which included eminent personalities from various nations.

The implementation of conciliar reforms met opposition from conservatives, such as Mgr. Lefèbvre, who provoked a schism in 1988 on the grounds that the liturgical reforms, episcopal collegiality, and the definition of religious liberty contradicted Church tradition as defined by the Council of Trent. At the other extreme, a number of progressive thinkers upheld the Council to outdo it, producing confusion among Catholics. In reality the positive effects of Vatican II are still much in evidence thirty years after the event. The papacy enjoys enormous prestige and attracts immense audiences from all over the globe. In the wake of the important trips of Paul VI, the travels of John Paul II have mobilized whole populations and have exerted incalculable ecclesiastical and political influence. Today Catholic vitality is best impressively reflected in those young Christian churches who have enthusiastically embraced the program of Vatican II.

The brief introduction to the pastoral constitution *Gaudium et Spes*, which is here reproduced, bears ample evidence to the content, aim, depth, and solicitude behind the Church's program in the service of mankind, both present and future. In solidarity with mankind, the Church proposes an ongoing human dialogue in the light of the principles of the Gospel, which have inspired man over the past two millennia. Solidarity, respect, and love toward all mankind are the hallmarks of the Church's mission on earth.

GAUDIUM ET SPES

The joys and the hopes, the grief, and the anxieties of modern man, and especially the poor or in any way afflicted, are also the joys and the hopes, the grief, and the anxieties of the followers of Christ ... The community of Christians therefore feels truly and intimately linked with mankind and his history (n.1).

Modern man wonders with admiration at his own discoveries and potential, but he also frequently raises anxious questions about the current trend of the world, about the place and role of man within the universe, about the meaning of his individual and collective efforts, and also about the ultimate destiny of reality and humanity. Hence, giving witness and voice to the faith of the whole People of God gathered together by Christ, this Council can provide no more eloquent proof of its solidarity with the entire human family with which it is bound up, as well as its respect and love for that family, than by engaging with it in conversation about these various problems. The Council brings to mankind light kindled from the Gospel, and puts at its disposal those saving resources which the Church itself, under the guidance of the Holy Spirit, receives from her Founder. For the human person deserves to be preserved; human society deserves to be renewed (n. 3).

---

1. Pope John XXIII with Archbishop Montini of Milan, the future Paul VI.
2. The opening of Vatican Council II by John XXIII on October 11, 1962 in St Peter's Basilica, Rome.
3. Pope John Paul II.
4. Holy Week in Michoacan, Mexico City, showing the representation of Christ's entry into Jerusalem. Popular religiosity portrays Christian traditions through theatrical representations which involve the whole population as actors and spectators.

2

4

3

GLOSSARY

words in CAPITALS are cross references

Arians, Arianism   Trinitarian heresy of the 4th and 5th centuries that took its name from the teachings of the Alexandrian priest Arius, who cast doubts on the divinity of Christ. Arius asserted that the Father alone is eternal, and while the son is the foremost and most excellent among all creatures, he was only an instrument in the hands of the Father during creation. The son is the wisdom and the image of the Father, but is neither co-eternal nor consubstantial with him. The son was made flesh in the figure of Christ Jesus, dwelling within a human being of whom he was but the soul. This heresy was condemned by the Councils of Nicaea (325) and Constantinople (381). The Goths (Ostrogoths and Visigoths) were Arians but Clovis's conversion eradicated this doctrine from the west.

Benedict of Nursia   Founder of the Benedictine Order. He was born at Nursia around 480 and, after becoming a hermit and a monk within the community of Subiaco, founded the abbey of Monte Cassino in 529. There he composed the *Regula*, which became the rule followed by most monasteries during and after the Middle Ages. He died at Monte Cassino in 547.

Bogomils, Bogomilism   A Balkan variation of the heresy of the CATHARS, which was based on the two concepts of good and evil and which drew its inspiration from Paulicianism, a Near-Eastern Manichean movement. Hounded out of Bulgaria where it was spreading, Bogomilism filtered into Bosnia, Dalmatia, Slovenia, and, finally, Serbia. Byzantium continuously harassed the Bogomils until they finally disappeared around the 1400s.

Cathars, Catharism   A dualistic heresy of the 12th and 13th centuries, extremely widespread in France (Albigenses) and the Balkans. Rooted in Manichean and Gnostic beliefs, it was probably imported from the East by the Crusaders. The Catharist movement believed in two powers ruling over sky and earth, good and evil. The evil god is the creator of matter while the good god is the creator of the spirit and of light. Moreover they practiced a most austere morality that forbade sex and consumption of meat; they believed in a baptism of the spirit that was believed to lead the perfect ones along the path of salvation; and they disregarded the Church and the sacraments. Catharism tainted all Europe.

Christian Humanism   Christian humanism started with Pico della Mirandola (d. 1494), Marisilio Ficino (d. 1499), and Nicholas of Cusa (d. 1464) who had escorted the orthodox delegation during the Council of Florence in 1439. Christian humanism developed in the 16th century under professors of the *studia humanitatis*, who yearned for a return to the Bible, Christian antiquity, and the Greek and Latin classics, but were also conscious of the dangers of a return to paganism. Important examples are Thomas More (d. 1535), Erasmus (d. 1536), and Lefèvre d'Étaples (d. 1536). Their teachings characterize the century and were instrumental in a renewal of Catholicism.

Cistercians   Benedictine monks adhering to the reform of Cîteaux initiated by Bernard of Clairvaux. His reform upheld the rigorous observance of the Benedictine rule, the ideal of complete retirement from the world, and observance of total poverty. The golden age of this Order was reached in the 12th and 13th centuries, when the number of abbeys rose from 343 in 1153 to 694 in 1300. This Order spread throughout Europe and is dearly held by the Church.

Congregation   A community of priests, or male or female laypersons, living according to a rule of life. In Roman Catholicism a congregation can also refer to one of the Vatican organs responsible for the running of an administrative department (for example, the Congregation for Eastern Churches).

Crusades   Military expeditions by Western Christianity in an attempt to re-conquer Jerusalem after its sacking by Muslims in 1009 and their devastation of the Holy Sepulchre. The Crusades drew support from three factors: the great popularity of pilgrimages to Jerusalem, the demographic expansion in the Western world, and the emergent Christian Orders of knighthood. During the Council of Clermont (1095) Pope Urban II launched a campaign for Christians to brandish the cross in support of the appeal of Byzantine Emperor Alexander Comnenus. There were eight Crusades.

Deism   A natural religiosity based on the idea of a supreme being who does not exercise any influence on human behavior.

'Devotio Moderna'   A spiritual movement of the 14th and 15th centuries that enjoyed great popularity in Flanders and the Rhine valley. It originated among the groups of Brethren of the Common Life inspired by Rysbroeck and Thomas of Kempen (or à Kempis) of the CONGREGATION of the Canons Regular of St. Augustine. This devotion sought to foster attachment to the person of Christ, his passion, and the Holy Eucharist. In this regard, the classical text was *The Imitation of Christ* of Thomas à Kempis. Erasmus and Nicholas of Cusa were disciples of the Brethren of the Common Life of Deventer.

Febronianism   An ecclesiological concept embraced by the Luxembourg theologian Nicolas von Hontheim (1701-1790), who served as auxiliary bishop of Trier. In 1763, under the pseudonym Febronius (from which Febronianism is derived) he published a treatise on the rights of national bishops. He upheld on all-powerful episcopate that refuted the primacy of the pope over the council and appealed to lay princes to assume direction over religious matters in their countries.

Gallicanism   A doctrine diffused in France between the 15th and 19th centuries that asserted a certain autonomy of the French Church in its relations with Rome, and a number of rights by French kings in matters of ecclesiastical administration. In 1438 the Pragmatic Sanction of Bourges invested the king of France with rights over Church nominations. The conciliar decrees of Trent remained unrecognized under French law, which considered them a violation of Gallican rights. Gallicanism was finally defeated by the Vatican Council I and its precepts regarding the pope's teaching office.

Great Western Schism (1378-1417)   Following the return of the popes from Avignon to Rome in 1378, the cardinals elected two popes, Urban VI and Clement VII, both of whom were supported by different monarchs. Even the religious Orders and dioceses were divided. The cardinals then elected Alexander V, who was in turn substituted within a year by John XXIII (antipope). At Constance a council deposed John XXIII, and in 1417 elected Pope Martin V, thereby ending the 39-year-old schism.

Ideology   The science of ideas, especially those of the 18th century. Today the term is used, above all else, to denote any abstract theory beyond reality, such as positivist or Marxist ideologies. The term 'ideological systems' refers to philosophical systems that analyze the meaning of life.

Inculturization of the Gospel   A new theological concept, coined by Pope John Paul II in his encyclical *Slavorum Apostoli* (1985): '... the embodiment of the Gospel within indigenous cultures and the integration of these same cultures in the life of the Church.' Inculturization begins with the proclamation of the Gospel, which, together with the people who accept it, enjoys a primary role. The encounter of culture with Gospel leads to a creative response by man.

Inquisition   The 13th-century Inquisition was an investigative body for the maintenance of public order, with rules guaranteeing a fair hearing for the accused. It was adopted around 1230 to inquire into cases of matters of faith, in view of the threats posed by the CATHARS and the WALDENSES. By 1231 the Inquisition had evolved into a special tribunal for the judging of heretical crimes in Germany and Italy and, by 1233, also in France. After 1252 the Inquisition assumed the power of inflicting torture on those accused of heresy, prior to their being handed over to the secular tribunal. The Spanish Inquisition goes back to 1478 and was established on the initiative of the Spanish monarchs against Jewish and Muslim minorities.

Jansenism   Theological movement (from the late 16th to the 18th century) concerned with the controversy between free will and grace. Drawing from a pessimistic philosophy and emphasizing the profound corruptive influence of sin over man, Jansenists upheld a rigorous moral code, while stressing the act of faith. They differed from Protestants in their Eucharistic and Marian devotions. The controversy between Jansenists and the Jesuits was particularly bitter.

Josephism   Term used to denote the enlightened despotism of the Austrian Emperor Joseph II (1765-1790) who gathered all Churches under his supervision in order to control, administer, and reform them, disregarding all rights of the papacy. He was pitiless against monasteries and religious Orders, considering them useless.

'Kulturkampf' (Cultural Struggle)   The battle (1871-1878) waged by Chancellor Bismarck against German Catholics to stamp out Church influence over internal politics. It included the suppression of the Jesuits, the promulgation of the 'May Laws' (which established State supervision over the education of the future priests), the control of ecclesiastical jurisdiction, and compulsory civil marriage. The term is also used politically to denote any organized opposition against the Church's influence over the civil and social life of the State.

Laicism   Deriving from 'layman,' the term signifies a modern movement that opposes any overlapping, or indeed any relationship, between the spiritual and the temporal. In certain countries laicism expresses itself as a form of anticlericalism with de-Christianizing tendencies. This was, for example, the case in Germany between 1870-1900 with the KULTURKAMPF, and in France with the oppression of religious CONGREGATIONS. For Catholics laicism also means the legitimate distinction of powers between Church and State, based on mutual respect and tolerance. Vatican Council II pronounced itself clearly on such a relationship.

Modernist Crisis, Modernism   A reform movement (end of the 19th and beginning of the 20th century), which aimed at divesting Catholicism of those traditional elements deemed as obsolete, and replacing them with a way of thinking and of living compatible with the modern world. In his encyclical letter *Pascendi* (1907), Pius X condemned a number of doctrinal errors resulting from the unorthodox tenets of this widespread movement.

Positivism   Teaching of Auguste Comte (1798-1857) upholding positivist science as the sole valid philosophy. This doctrine drew its inspiration from the Enlightenment, which aimed to free man's intellect from religious illusions and to lead it back to the reality of experience. Before Comte, David Hume had criticized all religious beliefs. Now that the development of human sciences has slowed considerably, positivism has been relegated to its rightful place among the precise sciences by whom it is criticized.

Propagation of Faith, Congregation for   In 1622 Pope Gregory XV instituted the CONGREGATION *De Propaganda Fide* to spread Christianity in distant lands. Distancing itself from colonialism, the Church encouraged the formation of an indigenous clergy, established a missionary seminary in Rome, and a printing house for the publication of catechisms in different languages. It thus embarked on a program of INCULTURIZATION OF THE GOSPEL.

Quietism   A spiritual movement formed in reaction against the ascetic expressions to which the Counter Reformation had attributed too much importance. This 'charismatic' movement that encouraged 'quiet prayer' gave rise to heated debates in Italy and France. The Church was suspicious of this religious practice of the heart and its 'mysticism of pure love,' which considered as useless all human efforts in prayer and Christian life. Its condemnation in 1685 cast a shadow over Christian asceticism.

Reform of Gregory VII (d. 1085)   Archdeacon of Rome, elected pope in 1073, Hildebrand of Soana took the name of Gregory VII and dedicated himself to the reform of the Church, insisting on compulsory priestly celibacy and the independence of papal power. He instituted permanent ambassadors for the Holy See and resisted the German Emperor Henry IV. He implemented a great reform within the Church, thanks to the Cluniac and Cistercian revivals and to a reformed episcopate.

Secularization   This ambiguous and multi-faceted term describes the passage from a religious to a lay state, such as the transfer of an ecclesiastical right onto a lay owner; the demotion of a consecrated person to a lay state; the withdrawal of society from religious practice; the total dissolution of religious sentiment in the world; and the removal of religious influence from civil life and state education, until a state of complete desacralization is reached, whereby all religious concerns are ignored.

Social Catholicism   A 19th-century movement that originated among working-class poor people in the wake of the Industrial Revolution and the economic liberalism generated by the French Revolution. Priests and laypersons mobilized themselves to help the working classes. In France Frederick Ozanam (d. 1853) founded the Society of St. Vincent de Paul; in Germany Adolf Kolping (d. 1865) and William von Ketteler (1877) were the pioneers of social legislation and an established network of cooperative worker societies. Albert de Mun (d. 1914) and René de la Tour du Pin (d. 1924) set up Catholic worker circles; Léon Harmel (d. 1924) was the forerunner of social charitable patronage. In Italy Giovanni Bosco (d. 1888), Giuseppe Tovini (d. 1897), and Giuseppe Toniolo (d. 1918) upheld the social involvement of Catholics. In this regard the encyclical letter of Leo XIII *Rerum Novarum* (1981) was both a point of arrival and departure.

Vandals   Germanic tribes who inhabited the region between the Vistula and the Oder in the third century. In 407 they crossed the Rhine and plundered Gaul, reaching Spain in 409 and Africa in 429. Establishing themselves as masters of all North Africa and the sea, they ravaged the coasts of the Mediterranean. As ARIANS they persecuted Catholics. They were subdued by Emperor Justinian I in 533-534.

Waldenses   Toward 1170 a rich merchant from Lyon named Valdus founded a religious movement which proclaimed the need for evangelical poverty, the need for vernacular versions of the Gospel, and the abolition of the cult of saints and relics. Harassed by the INQUISITION, the Waldenses sought refuge in the Alpine valleys, embraced Protestantism, and then migrated into the Italian Alps. The Waldenses constitute the most numerous Protestant faction in Italy.

INDEX